One for Everyone

More Poems I Love

Compiled by

Kathleen Watkins

Gill Books

Gill Books
Hume Avenue
Park West
Dublin 12
www.gillbooks.ie

Gill Books is an imprint of M.H. Gill & Co.

978 0 7171 9023 2

Printed by CPI Group (UK) Ltd, Croydon, CRO 4YY

This book is typeset in Dolly Pro.
The paper used in this book comes from the wood pulp
of managed forests. For every tree felled, at least one
tree is planted, thereby renewing natural resources.

A CIP catalogue record for this book is available from
the British Library.

5 4 3 2

For Gay

CONTENTS

INTRODUCTION

So there I was, settling in to cocooning in early 2020, sitting in my chair reading the paper, when the phone rang. It was Nicki Howard from Gill Books. She was ringing to ask me to select another book of my favourite poems. It was such a lovely surprise to get the call.

To my right hand, where I was sitting, were my shelves of poetry books, so I immediately started to pull out books one after the other and read through them. What a great way to occupy my time during the days and weeks ahead, I thought, as I socially distanced myself from everybody. So I got to work. It was a labour of love.

I'd read a book through, pick out my favourite few poems, and then collect the best for a final selection. I am also including with my choices three pieces written for Gay by Brendan Kennelly, Rita Ann Higgins and his Sunday Lyric FM producer Eithne Hand, who is publishing her first collection this autumn. I am also including with his kind permission the beautiful piece written for Eamon Kelly by Sebastian Barry. He read it at the celebration of Eamon at the Abbey Theatre produced by John McColgan on 21 June 1998. On that occasion, I asked Sebastian for a copy and he gave me his own on the night.

My love of poetry came from the nuns at my Dominican convent boarding school. The nuns were just extraordinary; amazing, really! When you're sowing a seed with a child in school you never know where it will end up. I will never forget Sr Angela in the music room explaining how to control our breath when we were learning to sing. She told us, 'If you can say it, you can sing it!' And so we did.

We did a musical play in school based on Moore's melodies (there are over seventy). It was simply beautiful. We all learned to play the harp, and we all had titles – I was Tradition, someone else was Culture, etc.

But the nuns taught us more than just the melodies. We were learning not just the music and how to perform it, but so much more. The love of words and music came to me there. I learned how to rehearse something without having the music in front of you, if you can just picture it in your mind.

Sr Angela gave me an appreciation for the rhythm of poetry and the flow. She showed me how to appreciate light and shade – that you can sandwich something serious in between a lighter piece so that everything doesn't have the same rhythm or tone. You put a slower air sandwiched between two quick airs.

I thought of her advice as I worked on this collection. I would go away from the selection of poetry, then come back and I could see the faults. It was like creating a flower arrangement, and I had to choose what flowers fitted best.

The joy of a collection is that you can dip into it at any time and select any poem. I hope I have captured an entertaining bunch that people can enjoy, full of family and real things that people experience as part of their lives.

CALLING THE KETTLE
DENNIS O'DRISCOLL

No matter what news breaks,
it's impossible to think straight
until the kettle has been boiled.

The kettle with its metal back
strong enough to take the strain,
shoulders broad enough to cry on;

plump as the old grandmother
in her woollen layers of skirts
who is beyond surprise or shock,

who knows the value of allowing
tears to flow, of letting off steam,
of wetting the tea and, her hand

patting your cheek, insisting – as she
prevails on you to sit and drink – that
things could have been much worse.

THE *DARLING* LETTERS
CAROL ANN DUFFY

Some keep them in shoeboxes away from the light,
sore memories blinking out as the lid lifts,
their own recklessness written all over them. *My own ...*
Private jokes, no longer comprehended, pull their
    punchlines,
fall flat in the gaps between endearments. *What
are you wearing?*

    Don't ever change.
They start with *Darling*; end in recriminations,
absence, sense of loss. Even now, the fist's bud flowers
into trembling, the fingers trace each line and see
the future then. *Always ...* Nobody burns them,
the *Darling* letters, stiff in their cardboard coffins.

Babykins ... We all had strange names
which make us blush, as though we'd murdered
someone under an alias, long ago. *I'll die*

without you. Die. Once in a while, alone,

we take them out to read again, the heart thudding

like a spade on buried bones.

DAD
ADAM WYETH

I'll always remember those Sunday drives home.
How a blackening silence came over us
with the night. I'd look back at the road
we'd set out on when our weekend had begun:

singing songs, stopping at petrol stations
in the back of beyond, turning off the beaten
track and finding a pub for lunch –
with swings and climbing frames to play on.

But all that was fading fast, as signs marked
the dwindling miles, oncoming headlights
dazzled us, the final catseyes blinked past
and the road emptied – losing its nerve

as we curved off the motorway. Then the real
darkness set in – the chill of parting
making me numb. I'd run upstairs to my room

without a word spoken, and from the corner

of my window watch your silver *Citroen* slip
into the night; a final sliver of light then total eclipse.
Another week of staring into space in classrooms,
waiting for our next outing all together. Save mum.

AFTER A CHILDHOOD AWAY FROM IRELAND

EAVAN BOLAND

One summer
we slipped in at dawn,
on plum-coloured water
in the sloppy quiet.

The engines
of the ship stopped.
There was an eerie
drawing-near,

a noiseless coming head-on
of red roofs, walls,
dogs, barley stooks.
Then we were there.

Cobh.
Coming home.

I had heard of this:
the ground the emigrants

resistless, weeping,
laid their cheeks to,
put their lips to kiss.
Love is also memory.

I only stared.
What I had lost
was not land
but the habit of land:

whether of growing out of,
or settling back on,
or being
defined by.

I climb

to your nursery.

I stand listening

to the dissonances

of the summer's day ending.

I bend to kiss you.

Your cheeks

are brick pink.

POEM FROM A THREE-YEAR-OLD
BRENDAN KENNELLY

And will the flowers die?

And will the people die?

And every day do you grow old, do I
grow old, no I'm not old, do
flowers grow old?

Old things – do you throw them out?

Do you throw old people out?

And how you know a flower that's old?

The petals fall, the petals fall from flowers,
and do the petals fall from people too,
every day more petals fall until the
floor where I would like to play I

want to play is covered with old
flowers and people all the same
together lying there with petals fallen
on the dirty floor I want to play
the floor you come and sweep
with the huge broom.

The dirt you sweep, what happens that,
what happens all the dirt you sweep
from flowers and people, what
happens all the dirt? Is all the
dirt what's left of flowers and
people, all the dirt there in a
heap under the huge broom that
sweeps everything away?

Why you work so hard, why brush
and sweep to make a heap of dirt?
And who will bring new flowers?

And who will bring new people? Who will
bring new flowers to put in water
where no petals fall on to the
floor where I would like to
play? Who will bring new flowers
that will not hang their heads
like tired old people wanting sleep?
Who will bring new flowers that
do not split and shrivel every
day? And if we have new flowers,
will we have new people too to
keep the flowers alive and give
them water?

And will the new young flowers die?

And will the new young people die?

And why?

GIVEN

JANE CLARKE

At a market stall on Bantry square
the woman in blue-striped apron

tells me yoghurt making's a mystery,
no two batches taste the same.

Try as you might for consistency,
you're surprised by the spectrum of flavours

from barely acidic to bitter as sloes,
textures thicker than buttermilk

or thinner than consommé.
You question everything; the starter culture,

the milk, the heat of fermentation.
On a good day you savour the difference,

the way a mother looks at her children,

in wonder at what she's been given.

FRIENDSHIP
SEAN BROPHY

When I think of friends
I think of easy company
Of no masks, ever

I think of shared experience
That binds together

I think of judgement suspended
I think of understanding
Of walking in each other's shoes

I think of acceptance
Of what we are
I think of belief in what we try to be
In authenticity

I think of you and you and you

My friends,

My dear friends

I think of you.

KING
PAULA MEEHAN

When I came to your inner chamber

having fought through the ranks of shadowy petitioners

you gave me the glad eye and sent

a note by a trusted courtier.

You promised a life of ease,

a place to work in peace,

songbirds and panthers, never

a worry about where the next meal was coming from,

no more hiding from the rent man, the ESB man,

the wolfman gnawing at my door.

And when you had me, burned me out,

you placed my ashes in your collection.

Number 8. A fine woman.

Pity about her accent though.

TO A CHILD
PATRICK KAVANAGH

Child, do not go
Into the dark places of the soul,
For there the grey wolves whine,
The lean grey wolves.

I have been down
Among the unholy ones who tear
Beauty's white robe and clothe her
In rags of prayer.

Child, there is light somewhere
Under a star.
Sometime it will be for you
A window that looks
Inward to God.

LOVE AFTER LOVE
DEREK WALCOTT

The time will come
when, with elation,
you will greet yourself arriving
at your own door, in your own mirror,
and each will smile at the other's welcome,

and say, sit here. Eat.
You will love again the stranger who was your self.
Give wine. Give bread. Give back your heart
to itself, to the stranger who has loved you

all your life, whom you ignored
for another, who knows you by heart.
Take down the love letters from the bookshelf,

the photographs, the desperate notes,
peel your image from the mirror.
Sit. Feast on your life.

FOR A NEW GRANDDAUGHTER

For Elizabeth Anne

ANNE LE MARQUAND HARTIGAN

So you have been born, my little one,
Alone you braved the rapids, alone
You made that dark journey
Hearing the familiar and the strange.

Out you are now fallen, among friends.
Your mother panting and your father
Holding your hand. They untie you,
And there you are, spitting

The unfamiliar out of your mouth,
Turning for the breast now you are cordless.
Your parents are as new as you,
Breathless they take names from a hat,

You are so yourself it is an imposition
To name you, but they will, and so
Move you from these first days of magic

Into the ordinary. To join us here.

You link us with dream, with eternity,
With everlasting, we can all live more
Clearly, for a little while,
Because you have arrived.

INSANITY VIEW
CIARAN O'DRISCOLL

I live at No 1 Insanity View,

and Freddie Bottomly's next door to me at No 3.

He has a goatee beard and recently

he bought a wheelbarrow.

"Nice wheelbarrow," I say,

and he grins with childish delight.

I'll murder him some night.

And I'll kill and eat old Mrs Fox

who lives across the road at No 2

and thought of nothing, towards the end of the war,

only the V-2

and whether it would blast her window box

of petunias and primulas

into eternity. And of course

there's Mr and Mrs Wilberforce

living at No 4

with their three nasty children

who knock at my front door
and run: I fancy they're tougher to chew
than Mr Bottomly's wheelbarrow,
but I'll kill and eat them too.
Aye, and everybody else
who lives on Insanity View.

THE 'SINGER'
MEDBH MCGUCKIAN

In the evenings I used to study
at my mother's old sewing-machine,
pressing my feet occasionally
up and down on the treadle
as though I were going somewhere
I had never been.

Every year at exams, the pressure mounted –
the summer light bent across my pages
like a squinting eye. The children's shouts
echoed the weather of the street,
a car was thunder,
the ticking of a clock was heavy rain....

In the dark I drew the curtains
on young couples stopping in the entry,
heading home. There were nights
I sent the disconnected wheel

spinning madly round and round

till the empty bobbin rattled in its case.

SPECIAL OFFER

For Jennie

GERRY GALVIN

When you were two and three and four,
we commandeered a trolley by the door;
you, my special offer, I propelled
between the lines of cereals, spices, jams,
two-for-one the relish and the ham.

Along the aisles of cans and creams
we cut a dash, careered past cabbages
and plums; we slowed – a bit –
before the frosty stares of those
who thought the place belonged to them.

That stuffy manager stopped us in our tracks.
'This is not a playground, sir!'
You stunned him with your outrage,
oh yes you did, you snapped,
'Bad man, must not be nasty to my dad!'
How we made our trolley dance

to the playfulness of this romance,

stocking up for one day hence

on the way to independence.

TERRORIST'S WIFE
ANGELA GREENE

A phone-call takes him
into the dark for weeks.
In the mornings, his absence
fills me with dread. I thin my eyes
to watch for cars that come to wait
down in the strect. All day
I move from room to room. I polish
each spotless place
to a chill shining. Fear tracks me
like hunger. In the silence,
the walls grow wafer-thin.
The neighbours wear masks—
tight lips, veiled looks, such
finc tissues of knowing.
my mother doesn't visit. I drag
My shopping from the next town.

Once, putting his clean shirts away,
my dry hands touched a shape
that lay cold and hard. I wept then,
and walked for hours in the park.
I listened for his name in the news.
When I looked at our sleeping son
my sadness thickened.
His comings are like his goings—
a swift movement in the night.

At times he can sit here for days
meticulously groomed; primed,
watching soccer games on TV,
our child playful on his lap.
Burt scratch the smooth surface
of his mood, and how
the breached defences spit their fire.

Now, when he holds me to him,

I know I taste murder

on his mouth. And in the darkness,

when he turns from me, I watch him

light a cigarette. In his palm

the lighter clicks and flames.

Balanced, incendiary.

BENEDICTION
JOE KANE

At sixty my mother still admired
his feet, long, slender and delicate:
pulling off his boots, the
smell of silage filled the kitchen.

Peeling first the right sock,
stroking, now the left,
pale and unblemished,
nails clear and straight.

Shaking her head at
this perfection, taking
his hands for comparison.
weathered, scarred and worn

From years spent wrestling
barbed wire and bullocks.

touches her back.

Are ye ready for your dinner?

LOVESICK
CAROL ANN DUFFY

I found an apple.
A red and shining apple.
I took its photograph.

I hid the apple in the attic.
I opened the skylight
and the sun said *Ah!*

At night, I checked that it was safe,
under the giggling stars,
the sly moon. My cool apple.

Whatever you are calling about,
I am not interested.
Go away. You with the big teeth.

AT THE RAILWAY STATION, UPWAY

THOMAS HARDY

"There is not much that I can do,

For I've no money that's quite my own!"

Spoke up the pitying child—

A little boy with a violin

At the station before the train came in,—

"But I can play my fiddle to you,

And a nice one 'tis, and good in tone!"

The man in the handcuffs smiled;

The constable looked, and he smiled, too,

As the fiddle began to twang;

And the man in the handcuffs suddenly sang

With grimful glee:

"This life so free

Is the thing for me!"

And the constable smiled, and said no word,

As if unconscious of what he heard;

And so they went on till the train came in —

The convict, and boy with the violin.

TO MY MOTHER
EITHNE STRONG

Just before sleep last night
I remembered.

Little woman
bearer of big men.

And before sleep
with knowledge near to tears
I knew again your fight.

Saw
the tired body sit so straight
while hands went on mending
into the late night.

Saw
the weary head
yet firm because of the strong will

bend over books that had to be known
for school on the morrow.

Knew
with surer knowing
your unflinching wrestle
with careful spending
of the much-earned wage.

Remembered
the special care of little things:
for grace of summer curtains
or flowers gathered in still busy
interlude from imperative chores–
remembered, now humble, and with praise.

Remembered too
the slight body in vivid action

against encroaching weeds,
impotently militant against
frequent defeat by horse and cow
in your limited domain.

As mothers live, and see
their children pass from them,
unknowing, I knew your grief.

And now
on hearing great music
tears run and run
for this and this.

I have lived these years
and know but now
pain of mothers
amid their children's going.

BROWN PENNY
WILLIAM BUTLER YEATS

I whispered, 'I am too young,'
And then, 'I am old enough';
Wherefore I threw a penny
To find out if I might love.
'Go and love, go and love, young man,
If the lady be young and fair.'
Ah, penny, brown penny, brown penny,
I am looped in the loops of her hair.

O love is the crooked thing,
There is nobody wise enough
To find out all that is in it,
For he would be thinking of love
Till the stars had run away
And the shadows eaten the moon.
Ah, penny, brown penny, brown penny,
One cannot begin it too soon.

GHOST STORIES
EAVAN BOLAND

Our American Hallowe'en was years ago.

    We wore

anoraks and gloves

and stood outside to watch

the moon above Iowa. Before dark,

I walked out

through the parking lot and playground

to our apartment block.

On every porch, every doorstep, candles

    fluttered in

pumpkins in the dusk on the eve

of the holiday. We

were strangers

there. I remember how our lighted rooms

looked through curtains from the road:

with that fragility.

DEATH OF A FARMER

GABRIEL FITZMAURICE

You pitched bales
Like a child tossing a coin;
You were sprightly as a dancer
When you swung the *sleán*.

Men boasted that they drank with you
At a fair;
You built a Gallarus
When you ricked turf and hay.

Your barns ring with birdsong,
There tramp and lovers lie;
But who will milk the cattle now
And cut the Winter's fire?

You were firm as bedrock,
Gnarled as bog oak,

Constant as spring water,
Wily as porter.

Alone you are and childless:
I grope by your side.
I will wash you, comb your hair,
And close your eyes.

PROMISE
LEANNE O'SULLIVAN

The grey sound of rain on the roof,
sound and light splitting on my skin
like flint pieces working me; I am preparing
a place for you, cleaning down the walls
and worktops, making space in the wide rooms,
in the small rooms, doubling things needed.
Roses I found growing around the bridge
I lay on your pillow; though time and love
go round like dancers, in time I won't be able
to tell your name from mine, to separate
your voice from my voice within this house.
My love I am at the table, waiting.
When you come home my hands shake
like rain breaking on the knotted waves.

FRIDAY
DENIS O'DRISCOLL

We are driving home.
Work is over, the weekend ours
like a gift voucher
to spend as we feel inclined.

We pass the armed guard
of whitethorn, the guard
of honour of poplars,
until our favourite

half-mile stretch
where a canopy of branches
spans the road
like a triumphal arch.

Our car tunnels into
this leafy underpass,

entering its funnel,

its decompression chamber.

Sheep are shearing fields;

lambs bound like woolly dogs

just released from the leash.

We have squeezed through

the filter of trees

and now, renewed, detoxified,

we are on the downward

slope towards home.

BUYING WINKLES
PAULA MEEHAN

My mother would spare me sixpence and say,
'Hurry up now and don't be talking to strange
men on the way.' I'd dash from the ghosts
on the stairs where the bulb had blown
out into Gardiner Street, all relief.
A bonus if the moon was in the strip of sky
between the tall houses, or stars out,
but even in rain I was happy – the winkles
would be wet and glisten blue like little
night skies themselves. I'd hold the tanner tight
and jump every crack in the pavement,
I'd wave up to women at sills or those
lingering in doorways and weave a glad path through
men heading out for the night.

She'd be sitting outside the Rosebowl Bar
on an orange-crate, a pram loaded
with pails of winkles before her.

When the bar doors swung open they'd leak
the smell of men together with drink
and I'd see light in golden mirrors.
I envied each soul in the hot interior.

I'd ask her again to show me the right way
to do *it*. She'd take a pin from her shawl –
'Open the eyelid. So. Stick it in
till you feel a grip, then slither him out.
Gently, mind.' The sweetest extra winkle
that brought the sea to me.
'Tell yer Ma I picked them fresh this morning.'

I'd bear the newspaper twists
bulging fat with winkles
proudly home, like torches.

WELCOME TO MY HEAD, please remove your boots
PAT INGOLDSBY

Lady Violet Netherington-Springs

sometimes wonders at the things

that hide and huddle underneath her bed,

but so long as they behave,

trim their toe-nails,

wash and shave,

nothing very much is ever said.

Lady Violet Netherington-Springs

has never seen the things

that hide and huddle underneath her bed,

but she hears them winding clocks,

grooming horses,

darning socks,

and she smells them baking home-made soda-bread.

Lady Violet Netherington-Springs

has no objection to the things,

that hide and huddle underneath her bed,

but now they're felling trees,

raising goats and keeping bees,

she feels it's time

that something firm was said.

Lady Violet Netherington-Springs

has reasoned with the things

that hid and huddled underneath her bed,

but she was gentle, kind and soft,

now they're all tucked in aloft,

and she hides and huddles underneath instead.

BLESSINGS
FRANCIS HARVEY

Yesterday, for some reason I couldn't
understand, I suddenly felt starved of
trees and had to make tracks towards
the beeches of Lough Eske to set my heart
at ease and stand there slowly adjusting
myself to the overwhelming presence of all
those trees. It was like coming back among
people again after living for ages
alone and as I reached out and laid my
right hand in blessing on the trunk of
a beech that had the solidity but not
the coldness of stone I knew it for
the living thing it was under the palm
of my hand as surely as I know the living
sensuousness of flesh and bone and my
blessing was returned a hundredfold
before it was time for me to go home.

RADIO DAYS

KATHLEEN BLANCHFIELD

The little wooden wireless
With its golden mesh-like front
Was where I first heard melodies,
Speeches, songs and chants.

I loved that little wireless
When I was just a child;
I listened to so many things.
I imagined men inside.

As I grew to teenage years
I was fascinated more
By the lovely Irish music
That made us take the floor.

Then, when I was just eighteen,
A transistor became mine –

A present for my birthday
From a boy I knew so fine.

A great transistor radio
Red and gold and white;
I felt I'd got a fortune
And listened day and night.

To Horace Batchelor in praise
Of his 'Station of the Stars';
O, twixt Luxembourg and Eireann
We had news from near and far.

That radio is still my own,
I'm married to the giver;
Michael and the radio –
I'll love them both forever.

FAREWELL
THOMAS MOORE

Farewell, but whenever you welcome the
> hour
That awakens the night-song of mirth in
> your bower,
Then think of the friend who once welcom'd
> it too,
And forgot his own griefs to be happy with
> you.
His griefs may return, not a hope may
> remain,
Of the few that had brighten'd his pathway of
> pain,
But he ne'er will forget the short vision that
> threw,
Its enchantment around him, while ling'ring
> with you.

And still on that evening when pleasure fills
 up,

To the highest top sparkle each heart and
 each cup,

Where 'ere my path lies, be it gloomy or
 bright,

My soul, happy friends, shall be with you
 that night.

Shall join in your revels, your sports, and
 your wiles,

And return to me beaming, all o'er with your
 smiles.

Too, blest if it tells me that 'mid the gay
 cheer,

Some kind voice had murmer'd, "I wish he
 were here!"

Let Fate do her worst, there are relics of joy,

Bright dreams of the past, which she cannot
destroy,

Which come in the night-time of sorrow and
care,

And bring back the features that joy used to
wear.

Long, long be my heart with such memories
fill'd,

Like the vase in which roses have once been
distill'd.

You may break, you may ruin the vase if you
will,

But the scent of the roses will hang 'round it
still.

SEÁN
MICHAEL PATTWELL

The first time I saw you
Your almost black hair
Was tinged with streaks of burnished gold
And you lay in another's arms.
A trace of a smile
Twitched the corners of your mouth
When you looked at me.
I felt at that moment
That you were special.

And you are.
The swallows under the eaves
Have come and hatched
And fledged and flown
Nine times.
For nine summers we've watched
Cygnets shed their drab brown
For dazzling white

And fly to other lakes
To other sea-shores.
Nine times the brown fields
Have turned green, then brown again,
Then into golden stubble.
For nine short years I've watched you grow.
I've watched you fall asleep at night.
I've watched you rise again refreshed
With each new sun.

Sometimes
You call me by my name,
Sometimes
You call me "Daddy",
But I will always
Call you
my son.

WHILE YOU ARE TALKING
MICHEAL O'SIADHAIL

While you are talking, though I seem all ears,
forgive me if you notice a stray see-through
look; on tiptoe behind the eye's frontiers
I am spying, wondering at this mobile you.
Sometimes nurturer, praise-giver to the male
caresser of failures, mother earth, breakwater
to my vessel, suddenly you'll appear frail –
in my arms I'll cradle you like a daughter.
Now soul-pilot and I confess redemptress,
turner of new leaves, reshaper of a history;
then the spirit turns flesh – playful temptress
I untie again ribbons of your mystery.
You shift and travel as only a lover can;
one woman and all things to this one man.

'IF I WAS A LADY'

PERCY FRENCH

If I was a lady, I'd wear a hat
That all the street would be lookin' at,
An' I'd have a ladies' maid, d'ye mind,
To lace and button me dress behind.
A dress that was lined with good sateen,
None o' yer bits o' bombazine.
And the girls with envy would grind their teeth,
When they heard it rustling underneath.
If I was a lady – but then I'm not,
This shawl is the dacentest thing I've got.

If I was a lady I'd drive to the play,
An' I'd look through me opera glass and say –
"I've seen this silly revue before,
The leading lady's an awful bore;
Let's all get up when she starts her song,
An' go an' eat cakes in a resterong."
Then a powder puff on me nose I'd dab,

An' drive off home in a taxi cab,

If I was a lady – but then I'm not,

A pass to the gallery's all I've got.

If I was a lady – a regular swell,

With a hairy boa, an' a silk umbrel'

'Tis me that would walk into Shelbourne's Hotel,

An' order me dinner – "Some pork an' beans,

An' whatever ye've got in them soup turreens,

Both the sweets, an' a hunk o' cheese,

And oh, a bottle o' porter please."

Then I'd call for me bill and setteling it,

I'd give the waiter a threepenny bit,

If I was a lady – but then I'm not,

My dinner comes out o' the stirabout pot.

Still there's a lot of show and sham,

Maybe I'm safer the way I am.

THE CHIMNEY SWEEP
JOHN SHEAHAN

A spread of old newspapers around the hearth,
And we knew he was expected. From early
   morning
We'd be on the lookout – black
As an engine driver, white-eyed under a sooty
   cap,
Stiff-bristled brushes strapped to the crossbar
   of the bike,
Ready for battle with the flue-lined waste
Of winter fires. *Mammy, the chimney sweep*
   is here!

"Ah! That was a hardy winter, Mam.
It'll be a tough job this time – " (An early hint
For a bigger tip.) "I see you're ready for me;
You can't bate the ould newspapers."

A soot-stained cloth with a hole in the
    middle
To mask the opening, and the black
    puppeteer
Was ready to perform. Up into the unknown
Went the first bristled head, and we watched,
    mesmerised,
As the hungry flue gobbled up one rod after
    another.

Coaxing it round an awkward bend,
He'd close his eyes, plotting the course in his
    head
Like a surgeon operating on a hidden organ.
Then with a subtle twist, he'd grunt it free.
"Must be the foreign coal," he'd mutter to
    himself.

"Should be coming out soon."

And we'd run outside and look up.

It's coming out! – the bristles vibrating with
　　freedom,

The black puppet nodding in the dazzling
　　daylight.

A CURIOUS GHOST

DEREK MAHON

While your widow clatters water into a kettle
you lie at peace in your southern grave –
a sea captain who died at sea, almost.
Lost voyager, what would you think of me,
husband of your fair daughter but impractical?
You stare from the mantelpiece, a curious ghost
in your peaked cap, as we sit down to tea.
The bungalows still signal to the sea,
rain wanders the golf-course as in your day,
the river still flows past the distillery
and a watery sun shines on Portballintrae.

I think we would have had a lot in common –
alcohol and the love of one woman
certainly; but I failed the eyesight test
when I tried for the Merchant Navy,
and lapsed into this lyric lunacy.

When you lost your balance like Li Po
they found unfinished poems in your sea-chest.

THE PIETA
PAUL BALFE

I had seen it before

But only ever on the page.

Nothing, but nothing

Can prepare you for

Its breath-taking beauty, its sheer magnificence.

How cold, hewn stone could capture such

passion,

Such profound emotion.

And yet it does.

Death was real death,

Desolation real desolation.

I'm humbled and awe struck

And sense the same

In the other onlookers.

Across the centuries, he's stirred our emotions –

The artist's ultimate triumph.

And his age?

Twenty-four.

WHEN LIFE STOPPED

(ex tenebris lux)

CATHERINE SWEENEY

And how was it
When life stopped?
And we were alone.
And we were old.
And we were confined.
And life was dark.

Then skies cleared.
And we saw the flowers.
And we heard the birds.
And life was bright.

And both these lives
Were how it was.
When life stopped.

And we missed the children.
And we were dependent.

And we served no purpose.
And life was dark.

Then family came.
And gifts at the closed door.
And friends zoomed.
And life was bright.

And all these lives
Were how it was.
When life stopped.

And tempers frayed.
And small things chafed.
And gratitude died.
And life was dark.

But love survived.

And appreciation returned.

And negativity was buried.

And life was bright.

And love survived.

And we were loved.

And we were cared for.

And we were grateful.

And all these lives

Were how it was.

When life stopped.

And brightness overcame the dark

When life stopped.

YOU DON'T GET TO BE RACIST AND IRISH

IMELDA MAY

You don't get to be racist and Irish

You don't get to be proud of your heritage,

plights and fights for freedom

while kneeling on the neck of another!

You're not entitled to sing songs

of heroes and martyrs

mothers and fathers who cried

as they starved in a famine

Or of brave hearted

soft spoken

poets and artists

lined up in a yard

blindfolded and bound

Waiting for Godot

and point blank to sound

We emigrated

We immigrated

We took refuge

So cannot refuse

When it's our time

To return the favour

Land stolen

Spirits broken

Bodies crushed and swollen

unholy tokens of Christ, Nailed to a tree

(That) You hang around your neck

Like a noose of the free

Our colour pasty

Our accents thick

Hands like shovels

from mortar and bricklaying

foundation of cities

you now stand upon

Our suffering seeps from every stone

your opportunities arise from

Outstanding on the shoulders

of our forefathers and foremothers

who bore your mother's mother

Our music is for the righteous

Our joys have been earned

Well deserved and serve

to remind us to remember

More Blacks

More Dogs

More Irish.

Still labelled leprechauns, Micks, Paddys, louts

we're shouting to tell you

our land, our laws

are progressively out there

We're in a chrysalis

state of emerging into a new

and more beautiful Eire/era

40 Shades Better

Unanimous in our rainbow vote

we've found our stereotypical pot of gold

and my God it's good.

So join us ... 'cause

You Don't Get To Be Racist And Irish.

MY SISTER IS NOT A STATISTIC
DOROTHY DUFFY

Tomorrow, when the latest Deathometer of Covid is
    announced in sonorous tones,
Whilst all the bodies still mount and curl towards the
    middle of the curve
Heaped one atop and alongside the other
My sister will be among those numbers, among the
    throwaway lines
Among the platitudes and lowered eyes,
an older person with underlying health conditions,
A pitiful way to lay rest the bare bones of a life.

My sister is not a statistic

Her underlying conditions were
Love
Kindness
Belief in the essential goodness of mankind
Uproarious laughter

Forgiveness

Compassion

A storyteller

A survivor

A comforter

A force of nature

And so much more

My sister is not a statistic

She died without the soft touch of a loved
    one's hand
Without the feathered kiss upon her
    forehead
Without the muted murmur of familiar family
    voices gathered around her bed,
Without the gentle roar of laughter that
    comes with memories recalled

Evoked from a time that already seems distant, when
    we were
connected by the simplicity of touch, of
    voice, of prcscnce.

My sister is not a statistic

She was a woman who spanned the seven ages.

A mother

A grandmother

A great grandmother

A sister

A friend

An aunt

A carer

A giver

My sister is not a statistic

And so, she joins the mounting thousands

They are not statistics on the Deathometer
    of Covid

They are the wives, mothers, children, fathers,
    sisters, brothers,
The layers of all our loved ones
If she could, believe me when I say, she would hold
    every last one of
your lost loves, croon to and comfort them and say
    – you were loved.
Whilst we who have been left behind mourn deep,
    keening the loss, the injustice, the rage.
One day we will smile and laugh again, we will
    remember with joy that,

once, we shared a life, we knew joy and survived sadness.

You are my sister ... and I love you.

THE ASH GROVE
JOHN OXENFORD

The ash grove, how graceful, how plainly 'tis
    speaking,
The wind [harp] through it playing has language
    for me.
Whenever the light through its branches is
    breaking
A host of kind faces is gazing on me.
The friends of my childhood again are before me,
Each step wakes a memory as freely I roam.
With soft whispers laden its leaves rustle o'er me,
The ash grove, the ash grove again [alone] is my
    home.

My laughter is over, my step loses lightness,
Old countryside measures steal soft on my ear;
I only remember the past and its brightness,
The dear ones I mourn [long] for again gather
    here.

From out of the shadows their loving looks
    greet me
And wistfully searching the leafy green
    dome,
I find other faces fond bending to greet me,
The ash grove, the ash grove alone is my
    home.

My lips smile no more, my heart loses its
    lightness
No dream of my future my spirit can cheer;
I only can brood on the past and its
    brightness,
The dead I have mourned are again living
    here.
From ev'ry dark nook they press forward to
    meet me;
I lift up my eyes to the broad leafy dome,

And others are there looking downward to
    greet me;
The ash grove, the ash grove alone is my
    home.

BOSS KELLY

For Eamon

SEBASTIAN BARRY

Who is that man as bright as a lamp
Fuming gently about the stage, the white hair
As fierce as fire? *It is Mr Kelly.*
And is he one of the Dublin Kellys –
No, listen to him talk, he has his own language,
Kerry, you know. How come
In the scene where he peels the plastic
Off the cheese for his brother's tea
His left leg rises of its own accord
Like one end of a branch snarled up
Underwater, the current pushing at it?
That comes under the heading
Of Acting. But how is it when he speaks
The lines, there is the singing parliament
Of wrens, rooks, and robins in them,
And, that when he mentions the waterfall
At the head of the Bunowen river
Not far from Droumagorteen

He somehow looks like that waterfall?

(and indeed, in the bright time after rain,

The hundred streams that make Hungry Hill

Resonate darkly.) It's a talent he has.

How come the pure water of his work

Is freaked with the whiskey of history? –

He is that sort of man. What sort is that? –

One that comes in a single packet

To the rich shop of life, who is unpacked

To the wonderment of the village.

Is it true then that Mr Kelly, as some say,

Is in league with another world,

That he is in fact the fiery father of the past,

The present and the future? *I expect.*

THE FIRST
(written for Gay's final GB show)
BRENDAN KENNELLY

You were the first to let the people speak their minds

You listened to what each one had to say

In your patient, tolerant, critical way.

Responding when they raised inquiring hands

To speak of pain or fun, of loss or gain.

You encouraged Ireland to open up

To face the ghost of darkness

Let them rip apart the secret heart

In sun and ice and rain.

You were a one-man university

Where all were welcome without paying a fee.

You gave us words, ideas, music, song

Often you made us laugh out loud and long

Beneath it all you searched for what was true

Thank you for that.

But thank you most of all for being you.

CLEARING THE LANE
i.m. GB
EITHNE HAND

Severed purple thistles
Tangle into living hedge,

Snipped rye grass rustles
Thin tunes skywards

While you are dying
I cut brambles, wait for rain.

MORTAL
(In memoriam Gay Byrne)
RITA ANN HIGGINS

Yes, he was loved

Adored and cherished.

He was a mortal, not a God.

He knew this better than most.

When night times came

And November folded itself around him,

And his slight shoulders,

He had the thoughts of a mortal.

He wondered what was next.

EVERYTHING IS GOING TO BE ALL RIGHT

DEREK MAHON

How should I not be glad to contemplate

the clouds clearing beyond the dormer window

and a high tide reflected on the ceiling?

There will be dying, there will be dying,

but there is no need to go into that.

The lines flow from the hand unbidden

and the hidden source is the watchful heart;

the sun rises in spite of everything

and the far cities are beautiful and bright.

I lie here in a riot of sunlight

watching the day break and the clouds flying.

Everything is going to be all right.

ABOUT THE POETS

Adam Wyeth is a poet, playwright and essayist. His debut collection, *Silent Music*, was Highly Commended by the Forward Poetry Prize. Adam's second book, *The Hidden World of Poetry*, contains poems from Ireland's leading poets followed by essays. His third book and second collection of poetry, *The Art of Dying*, was published in 2016 and was named as a book of the year in *The Irish Times*. Adam's plays have had several professional productions in Ireland, Berlin and New York. In 2014, he adapted his debut play *Hang Up* for the screen, which premiered at the Cork International Film Festival.

Angela Greene was born in England in 1936 and grew up in Dublin. She received the Patrick Kavanagh Award, in 1989 was shortlisted for The Sunday Tribune/Hennessy Literary Award, and was a prizewinner in the Bloodaxe Books National Poetry Competition in 1987. Her poetry was published in Britain and Ireland, read on RTE Radio and BBC Radio Ulster and was performed at the Project Arts Centre, Dublin. Her collection *Silence and the Blue Night* was published by Salmon Poetry in 1993.

Anne Le Marquand Hartigan is a prize-winning poet, playwright and painter. She trained as a painter at Reading University, England. She returned to Co. Louth in 1962 with her husband Tim Hartigan where they farmed and reared their six children. She now lives in Dublin. She has published seven collections of poetry, *Unsweet Dreams* (Salmon Poetry, 2011), *To Keep The Light Burning* (Salmon Poetry, 2008), *Nourishment* (Salmon Poetry, 2005), *Immortal Sins* (Salmon Poetry, 1993), *Now is a Moveable Feast* (Salmon Poetry, 1991), *Return Single* (Beaver Row Press, 1986) and *Long Tongue* (Beaver Row Press, 1982). Hartigan's prose work includes *Clearing the Space* (Salmon, 1996).

Brendan Kennelly was born in Co. Kerry in 1936. He has published over fifty books of poetry, including *My Dark Fathers* (1964), *Collection One: Getting Up Early* (1966), *Good Souls to Survive* (1967), *Dream of a Black Fox* (1968), *Love Cry* (1972), *The Voices* (1973), *Shelley in Dublin* (1974), *A Kind of Trust* (1975), *Islandman* (1977), *A Small Light* (1979) and *The House That Jack Didn't Build* (1982). He is also the author of two novels, *The Crooked Cross* (1963) and *Florentines* (1967) He was Professor of Modern Literature at Trinity College, Dublin for over 30 years, until he retired from the post in 2005.

Carol Ann Duffy is a British poet and playwright. She is a Professor of Contemporary Poetry at Manchester Metropolitan University, and was Poet Laureate from 2009–2019. Her collections include *Standing Female Nude* (1985), winner of a Scottish Arts Council Award; *Selling Manhattan* (1987), which won a Somerset Maugham Award; *Mean Time* (1993), which won the Whitbread Poetry Award; and *Rapture* (2005), winner of the T. S. Eliot Prize.

Catherine Sweeney is from Dublin. While cocooning with her husband during the COVID-19 pandemic, she began writing poetry as part of an artistic family project. 'When Life Stopped' reflects the darkness of the lockdown period but also the light provided by the love and support of family and friends and the arrival of spring in the garden.

Ciaran O'Driscoll was born in Co. Kilkenny in 1943 and now lives in Limerick. He has published eight books of poetry including *Moving On, Still There* (Dedalus Press, 2001) and more recently *Surreal Man*, a chapbook of 21 poems (Pighog, 2006), and *Vecchie Donne di Magione*, a dual-language edition of poems in an Italian setting (Volumnia Editrice, 2006). In 2001, Liverpool University

Press published his childhood memoir, *A Runner Among Falling Leaves*. He has won a number of awards for his work, among them the Patrick and Katherine Kavanagh Fellowship in Poetry. In 2007, he was elected to Aosdána.

Dennis O'Driscoll was an Irish poet and critic born in Co. Tipperary. His books include *Reality Check* (Copper Canyon Press, 2008), *New and Selected Poems* (Anvil Press, 2004), and *Troubled Thoughts, Majestic Dreams*, a collection of essays and reviews published by Gallery Press in 2001. He worked as a civil servant in Dublin.

Derek Mahon was born in Belfast in 1941, and now lives in Kinsale, Co. Cork. A member of Aosdána, he has received numerous awards including the Irish Academy of Letters Award, the Scott Moncrieff Translation Prize, and Lannan and Guggenheim Fellowships. His most recent books of poetry include *An Autumn Wind* (Gallery Press, 2010), *Life on Earth* (Gallery Press, 2008), *Somewhere the Wave* (Gallery Press, 2007), *Harbour Lights* (Gallery Press, 2005) and *Collected Poems* (Gallery Press, 1999). He also coauthored *In Their Element: A Selection of Poems* with Seamus Heaney (Arts Council of Northern Ireland, 1977).

Derek Walcott, born in 1930, was a West Indian poet and playwright. His collections include *In A Green Night* (1962), *Tiepolo's Hound* (2000), *The Prodigal* (2004), *White Egrets* (2010) and the epic poem *Omeros* (1990). Walcott's honours include a MacArthur Foundation Fellowship, the T.S. Eliot Prize, the Montale Prize, a Royal Society of Literature Award and the Queen's Medal for Poetry. In 1992, Walcott received the 1992 Nobel Prize in Literature, and in 2015, he received the Griffin Trust for Excellence in Poetry's Lifetime Achievement Award. He was an honorary member of the American Academy and Institute of Arts and Letters.

Dorothy Duffy was born in Co. Mayo and emigrated to England. When her sister Rose passed away in a London care home during the coronavirus pandemic, Dorothy wrote 'My Sister is not a Statistic' in her honour. The poem was broadcast on BBC and RTÉ and around the world as a tribute to Rose and all those who have lost their lives to COVID-19.

Eavan Boland was born in 1944 and is considered to be one of Ireland's most important contemporary poets. She was Professor of Humanities and Director of the Creative

Writing Programme at Stanford University, where she began teaching in 1996. Her collections include *Night Feed* (1982), *Outside History* (1990), *A Time of Violence* (1994, shortlisted for the T. S. Eliot Prize), *Against Love Poetry* (2001, New York Times Notable Book of the Year), *Domestic Violence* (2007) and *A Woman Without A Country* (2014).

Eithne Hand is an award-winning radio producer and writer from Greystones, Co. Wicklow. Her poetry was shortlisted for the Patrick Kavanagh award 2010, Hennessy New Irish Writing 2014 and the Gregory O'Donoghue award. She has been published in *The SHOp* and *The Stony Thursday Book*.

Eithne Strong was an Irish poet and writer born in Limerick in 1925. She wrote in both Irish and English and published many poetry collections, including *Fuill agus Fallaí* and *Songs of Living*, as well as two novels and a collection of short stories. She was a founding member of Runa Press and is commemorated by the Eithne and Rupert Strong Award.

Francis Harvey was an Irish poet and playwright. He was born in 1925 in Enniskillen, Co. Fermanagh, and lived in

Co. Donegal for most of his life. His collections of poetry include *In the Light on the Stones* (1978), *The Rainmakers* (1988), *The Boa Island Janus* (1996), *Making Space, New & Selected Poems* (2000), and *Collected Poems* (2007).

Gabriel Fitzmaurice was born in 1952 in Co. Kerry, where he still lives. For over 30 years he taught in the local primary school and retired as principal in 2007. He is the author of more than 60 books, including *Rainsong* (1984), collections of poetry in English and Irish as well as several collections of verse for children. He frequently broadcasts on radio and television on culture and the arts.

Gerry Galvin was born in Drumcollogher, Co. Limerick in 1942 and lived in Oughterard, Co. Galway. He was a chef and former restauranteur, author of two cookbooks, *The Drimcong Food Affair* (McDonald Publishing, 1992) and *Everyday Gourmet* (The O'Brien Press, 1997), and a columnist for *Organic Matters* magazine. His first volume of poems *No Recipe* was published in 2010, and his poetry and short stories were published widely in newspapers and magazines in both the UK and Ireland.

Imelda May was born in Dublin in 1974. A singer, song-writer and multi-instrumentalist, she has released five studio albums, *No Turning Back* (2003), *Love Tattoo* (2008), *Mayhem* (2010), *Tribal* (2014) and *Life Love Flesh Blood* (2017). In 2020, she released a spoken word album of poetry, *Slip of the Tongue*.

Jane Clarke grew up on a farm in Co. Roscommon and now lives with her partner in Glenmalure in Co. Wicklow. Her first collection, *The River*, was published by Bloodaxe Books in 2015. Her second collection, *When the Tree Falls*, was published by Bloodaxe Books in September 2019. *All the Way Home*, an illustrated sequence of poems in response to a soldier's letters from the Front during World War I, was published by Smith|Doorstop in April 2019, in collaboration with the Mary Evans Picture Library, London.

Joe Kane was born in Dublin in 1952. He studied ceramics and glass and he opened a studio in Donegal in 1976. In 2002 he completed an M.A. in Creative Writing (Poetry) with Lancaster University. His award-winning poems have been widely published. His collection *The Boy who Nearly Won the Texaco Art Competition* was published by New Island in 2007.

John Oxenford was born in 1812 and was an English dramatist, critic and translator. 'The Ash Grove' is a traditional Welsh folk song whose melody has been set to numerous sets of lyrics. The most well-known was written, in English, by Oxenford in the 19th century.

John Sheahan is one of Ireland's best-known musicians. Born in Dublin in 1939, he was a member of The Dubliners from 1964 to 2012. He has played with musicians the world over and has guested on numerous folk, traditional and rock recordings. His debut collection of poetry, *Fiddle Dreams*, was published by Dedalus Press in 2015.

Kathleen Blanchfield lives in Co. Kilkenny with her husband and daughters. Her poems have been published in magazines and newspapers and broadcast on radio. She is a keen gardener and works regularly with caring organisations. *The Paraffin Lamp* (2003) is her first book of poems.

Leanne O'Sullivan was born in 1983 in Co. Cork. She has published three collections from Bloodaxe Books, *The Mining Road* (2013), *Cailleach: The Hag of Beara* (2009) and *Waiting for My Clothes* (2004). Her work has been included in various anthologies, including *Best Irish Poetry 2010* (Southword Publishing), *The New Irish Poets* (Bloodaxe Books, 2004) and *Poetry 180: A Turning Back to Poetry* (Random House, 2003). Leanne was the recipient of the 2009 Ireland Chair of Poetry bursary and in 2010 was awarded the Rooney Prize for Irish Literature.

Medbh McGuckian was born in 1950 in Belfast, Northern Ireland, where she now lives with her family. She studied at Queen's University and later returned as their first female writer-in-residence. She is the author of over 20 poetry collections including most recently *Love, The Magician* (2018), *Blaris Moor* (2015), *The High Caul Cap* (2012) and *The Currach Requires No Harbours* (2010). Among the prizes she has won are England's National Poetry Competition, the Cheltenham Award, the Rooney Prize, the Bass Ireland Award for Literature, the Denis Devlin Award, the Alice Hunt Bartlett Prize, and, in 2002, the Forward Prize for Best Poem. She received the American Ireland Fund Literary Award in 1998 and an honorary Doctorate from the University of Aberdeen. She is a member of Aosdána.

Michael Pattwell was born in Clonakilty, Co. Cork and now lives in Ballinhassig. He has worked as a bakery worker, customs officer and a court clerk, business-man and a lorry driver. He took up the study of law as a mature student in 1971. He qualified as a solicitor in 1976 and ran his own practice in his hometown. He was appointed a judge of the District Court in 1990 and retired in June, 2011. He has been writing regularly for about twenty years. He published his first collection, *Flaghopping*, in 2010.

Micheal O'Siadhail was born in 1947. His collections of poetry include *Hail! Madam Jazz* (Bloodaxe Books, 1992), *A Fragile City* (Bloodaxe Books, 1995), *Our Double Time* (Bloodaxe Books, 1998), *The Gossamer Wall* (Bloodaxe Books and Time Being Books 2002), *Love Life* (Bloodaxe Books, 2005) and *Globe* (Bloodaxe Books, 2007). He has been a lecturer at Trinity College Dublin and a profes-sor at the Dublin Institute for Advanced Studies. He was a member of the Arts Council and the Advisory Committee on Cultural Relations and was a founding member of Aosdána. He was the founding chairman of Ireland Literature Exchange.

Pat Ingoldsby was born in 1942. An Irish poet and TV presenter, he has hosted children's TV shows, written plays for the stage and for radio, published books of short stories, and been a newspaper columnist. His radio plays include *The Dark Days of Denny Lacey*, *Fire is Far Enough* and *Liffey Ever Is*, all broadcast on RTÉ. Since the mid-1990s, he has been most widely known for his collections of poetry, which he sells on the streets of Dublin.

Patrick Kavanagh was born in a rural area of Co. Monaghan in 1904. The son of a shoemaker who owned a small farm, he left school at the age of twelve and taught himself about literature, becoming one of Ireland's most famous poets. His poetry collections include *The Great Hunger* (1971), *Come Dance With Kitty Stobling* (1960), *A Soul for Sale* (1947), and *Ploughman* (1936), and his most celebrated novel is *Tarry Flynn* (1948).

Paul Balfe grew up in Dublin in the 1960s. He studied Medicine at Trinity College Dublin and is currently a practicing surgeon at St. Luke's Hospital, Kilkenny. He was awarded the September 2016 Irish Times/Hennessy New Irish Writing award for poetry. His first collection, *Four Seasons*, was published by Salmon Poetry in 2019.

Paula Meehan was born in 1955 in Dublin where she still lives. She studied at Trinity College, Dublin, and at Eastern Washington University in the US. She has received many awards, including the Marten Toonder Award for Literature, The Butler Literary Award for Poetry, the Denis Devlin Memorial Award and the PPI Award for Radio Drama. She has published five collections of poetry, the most recent being *Painting Rain* (Carcanet, 2009). A selected volume, entitled *Mysteries of the Home*, was published in 1996. Her writing for stage includes the plays *Mrs Sweeney* (1997), *Cell* (1999), and, for children, *Kirkle* (1995), *The Voyage* (1997) and *The Wolf of Winter* (2003/2004). Meehan is a member of Aosdána, the Irish affiliation of writers and artists.

Percy French was born in Co. Roscommon in 1854. He was educated at Windermere College, Foyle College and Trinity College Dublin. He had a long and successful career as a songwriter and entertainer as well as a watercolour artist. He is remembered for such songs as 'Phil the Fluters Ball' and 'The Mountains of Mourne'.

Rita Ann Higgins was born in Galway. She has published ten collections of poetry, including *Ireland is*

Changing Mother (Bloodaxe, 2011) and *Tongulish* (Boodaxe, 2016), and a memoir in prose and poetry, *Hurting God* (Salmon, 2010). She is the author of six stage plays and one screenplay. She has been awarded numerous prizes and awards, among others an honorary professorship. She is a member of Aosdána.

Sean Brophy, a Dubliner, was born in 1943. His collections of poetry include *The Woman Next Door, The Awakening, Elegy, Girl Through My Window* and *Touching the Infinite*.

Sebastian Barry was born in Dublin in 1955. His novels and plays have won the Kerry Group Irish Fiction Prize, the Costa Book of the Year award, the Irish Book Awards Best Novel, the Independent Booksellers Prize and the James Tait Black Memorial Prize. He also had two consecutive novels, *A Long Long Way* (2005) and *The Secret Scripture* (2008), shortlisted for the MAN Booker Prize. He lives in Wicklow with his wife and three children.

Thomas Hardy was born in Dorset, England in 1840. As a novelist he is best known for his work set in the semi-fictionalized county of Wessex including *Tess* *of the d'Urbervilles* and *Jude the Obscure*. He was also an accomplished poet. From 1898 until his death in 1928 Hardy published eight volumes of poetry; about one thousand poems were published in his lifetime.

Thomas Moore was born in 1779 in Dublin and was a poet, singer, songwriter and entertainer. He was a prominent member of the nineteenth-century Gaelic revival and was a close friend of Lord Byron and Percy Bysshe Shelley. He is best remembered for the lyrics of 'The Minstrel Boy' and 'The Last Rose of Summer'.

William Butler Yeats was born in 1865 in Dublin to an Anglo-Irish Protestant family. Yeats' mother was from Co. Sligo, and his literature drew on the rich Irish folklore and iconic landscapes that he found there. Yeats' first book of poems, *The Wanderings of Oisin*, was published in 1889, and he went on to have a long career as a poet, playwright and critic, composing iconic works including 'The Second Coming', 'Lake Isle of Innisfree' and 'Easter, 1916'. Yeats was one of the founders of the Abbey Theatre in Dublin, and in 1923 he was awarded the Nobel Prize in Literature.

ACKNOWLEDGEMENTS

The publishers gratefully acknowledge permission to reprint copyright material in this book as follows:

'The Pieta' by Paul Balfe from *Four Seasons* (Salmon Poetry, 2019), reproduced with permission of Salmon Poetry.

'Boss Kelly' by Sebastian Barry, reproduced with permission of the author.

'Radio Days' by Kathleen Blanchfield from *The Paraffin Lamp* (Rectory Press, 2003), reproduced with permission of the author.

'After a Childhood Away from Ireland' and 'Ghost Stories' by Eavan Boland from *New Collected Poems* (Carcanet, 2005), reproduced with permission of Carcanet Press Limited, Manchester, UK.

'Friendship' by Sean Brophy from *The Awakening and Other Poems* (Rainsford Press, 1992).

'The *Darling* Letters' from *Love Poems* (Picador, 2010) and 'Lovesick' from *Selected Poems* (Penguin Books, 1994) by Carol Ann Duffy. Copyright © Carol Ann Duffy. Reproduced by permission of the author c/o Rogers, Coleridge & White Ltd., 20 Powis Mews, London W11 1JN.

'My Sister is Not a Statistic' by Dorothy Duffy, reproduced with permission of the author.

'Death of a Farmer' by Gabriel Fitzmaurice from *Rainsong* (Beavor Row Press, 1985), reproduced with permission of the author.

'Special Offer' by Gerry Galvin from *No Recipe* (Doire Press, 2010), reproduced with permission of Doire Press.

'Terrorist's Wife' by Angela Greene from *Silence and the Blue Night* (Salmon Poetry, 1993), reproduced with permission of Salmon Poetry.

'Clearing the Lane' by Eithne Hand from *Fox Trousers* (Salmon Poetry, 2020), reproduced with permission of Salmon Poetry.

'Blessings' by Francis Harvey from *Collected Poems* (Dedalus Press, 2007), reproduced with permission of Dedalus Press.

'Mortal' by Rita Ann Higgins, reproduced with permission of the author.

'WELCOME TO MY HEAD, please remove your boots' by Pat Ingoldsby from *Collected Poems of Pat Ingoldsby, introduced by Gay Byrne* (Rainbow Publications Ltd., Ireland, 1986), reproduced with permission of the author.

'Benediction' by Joe Kane from *The Boy who Nearly Won the Texaco Art Competition and other poems* (New Island, 2007), reproduced with permission of New Island.

'To A Child' by Patrick Kavanagh from *Collected Poems* (Penguin, 2005).

'Poem from a Three-Year-Old' by Brendan Kennelly from *Familiar Strangers: New & Selected Poems 1960-2004* (Bloodaxe Books, 2004), reproduced with permission of Bloodaxe Books. www.bloodaxebooks.com.

'The First' by Brendan Kennelly, special commission for Gay Byrne's final *Late Late Show*, RTÉ, reproduced with permission of the author.

'For a New Granddaughter' by Anne le Marquand Hartigan from *Immortal Sins* (Salmon Poetry, 1993), reproduced with permission of Salmon Poetry.

'Everything Is Going to Be All Right' and 'A Curious Ghost' by Derek Mahon from *New Collected Poems* (Gallery Press, 2011). By kind permission of the author and The Gallery Press, Loughcrew, Oldcastle, County Meath, Ireland.

'You don't get to be racist and Irish' by Imelda May, reproduced with permission of the author.

'Buying Winkles' and 'King' by Paula Meehan from *As If by Magic: Selected Poems* (Dedalus Press, forthcoming), reproduced with permission of Dedalus Press.

'The "Singer"' by Medbh McGuckian from *Selected Poems* (Gallery Press, 1997). By kind permission of the author and The Gallery Press, Loughcrew, Oldcastle, County Meath, Ireland.

'Insanity View' by Ciaran O'Driscoll from *Listening to Different Drummers* (Dedalus Press, 1993).

'Calling the Kettle' and 'Friday' by Dennis O'Driscoll from *Collected Poems* (Carcanet, 2017), reproduced with permission of Carcanet Press Limited, Manchester, UK.

'While You Are Talking' by Micheal O'Siadhail from *Collected Poems* (Bloodaxe Books, 2013), reproduced with permission of Bloodaxe Books. www.bloodaxebooks.com.

'Promise' by Leanne O'Sullivan from *Cailleach: The Hag of Beara* (Bloodaxe Books, 2008), reproduced with permission of Bloodaxe Books. www. bloodaxebooks.com.

'Séan' by Michael Patwell from *Flaghopping and Other Poems* (2014), reproduced with permission of the author.

'Chimney Sweep' by John Sheahan from *Fiddle Dreams: Poems and Lyrics* (Dedalus Press, 2015), reproduced with permission of Dedalus Press.

'To My Mother' by Eithne Strong from *Spatial Nosing* (Salmon Poetry, 2000), reproduced with permission of Salmon Poetry.

'When Life Stopped' by Catherine Sweeney, reproduced with permission of the author.

'Love after Love' by Derek Walcott from *The Poetry of Derek Walcott 1948-2013* (Faber & Faber, 2014), reproduced with permission of Faber & Faber.

'Dad' by Adam Wyeth from *Silent Music* (Salmon Poetry, 2011), reproduced with permission of Salmon Poetry.

The author and publisher have made every effort to trace all copyright holders, but if any have been inadvertently overlooked we would be pleased to make the necessary arrangement at the first opportunity.